To stay afloat.

Warmed By The Sun, Chilled By The Breeze

by Carla M. Cherry

iiPUBLISHING

Warmed By The Sun, Chilled By The Breeze
Copyright © 2025 by Carla M. Cherry

Cover design by tonii

ISBN: 979-8-9850204-8-9

Printed in the United States of America

iiPUBLISHING
New York, NY
www.toniiinc.com

Warmed By The Sun, Chilled By The Breeze

Water was our way here and it was my way back.

Acknowledgements

This chapbook emerged from my time with Brad Vogel's NYC Poets Afloat 2024, a micro-residency that began in 2019 endeavoring to match New York City poets with various ships across the city and allow them to spend time aboard writing poems. The poems are then shared during two readings, one in May, and one in June.

On May 19, 2024, the first reading for our cohort was held on the Tall Ship Wavertree at South Street Seaport in Manhattan, and on June 12, 2024, the second reading took place on the Mary Whalen in Red Hook, Brooklyn.

Although I was originally assigned to the City Island Sailboat, I was unable to coordinate my schedule with theirs in the Spring 2024. Luckily, I was reassigned to The Ambrose at South Street Seaport, and consequently, I was able to walk right over to visit The Tall Ship Wavertree and the South Street Seaport Museum. If you're a fan of maritime history, I encourage you to visit these sites and research their fascinating history.

Fortunately, Brad Vogel connected me with Neela Wickremesinghe, who generously arranged for me to spend time on *The Free Spirit*. With Fred Chandler's support, I was able to spend time in City Island Harbor, in my beloved Bronx, in the Fall 2024.

These poems were inspired by information I gleaned from my visits to these vessels, the South Street Seaport Museum, articles, and my own imagination.

I want to thank poet Brad Vogel, Coordinator of NYC Poets Afloat, for providing me with this amazing poetic experience; Zak Risinger, Director of Engagement and Public Programs at the South Street Seaport Museum, for his support and assistance; Caleb, my tour guide on the Ambrose; Neela K. Wickremesinghe, and Fred Chandler from Barron's Boatyard in the Bronx. I am also grateful to Nidhi Gandhi, my classmate at the City College of New York, for encouraging me to apply to NYC Poets Afloat.

And now, the poems.

CONTENTS

Part I: Looking Back

Part II: On the Ambrose

Part III: On the Wavertree

Part IV: The White Star Line

Part V: City Island Sailboat

PART I

LOOKING ING BACK

A Great Sorrow

Dear Mami Wata,

The Abby.
The Aggy.
The Africa.
The Ajax.
The Duc De Maine.
The Henrietta Marie.

Slavemasters
and overseers' whips.

Jim Crow and
acid attacks
to force us out of pools.

Poverty and
pool fees.

So many
of your daughters and sons

have not known,
do not know how to swim.

How often do you
cry?

Plunge

Summer.
I am four.
Donna, not quite two.
A drive South to see aunts and uncles and cousins.
This time we are staying at a hotel!
A pool!
I bounce in the back seat of the car and cheer.

After we change–
me into my navy blue one-piece with white polka dots–
we go downstairs, then outside.
Mommy is holding Donna,
Daddy is gathering chairs.

The water sparkles.
I can read,
but I do not look at the numbers
indicating depth.

This turquoise blue invites me
to cool off from this North Carolina sun.

I break away from them, run.
Jump in!

This turquoise blue feels good on my skin,
but I am sinking,
water over my head.

I think Mommy is screaming.
I look up.
Bubbles.
My flailing limbs.

How will I get out?

Daddy's arms around me.
There is sun and sky and air again.
I am on the pool's edge,

coughing and shivering
while Daddy gently pats my back.

I cannot remember
if we stayed at the pool after that,

but I never forgot

Daddy knows how to swim,
and Mommy does not.

Stuck in the Shallow End

Instead of swimming lessons during our field trips
to Mohansic State Park,

our camp counselors sat nearby on towels
sunning brown bodies to gleaming,
people watching and gossiping,
flirting,

as we jumped into the pool, squealing,
yelling at the boys to stop splashing us.

Me
Donna
Niecy
Tonya
formed a circle of safety.

Closed our eyes.
Held our noses.
Dropped to our knees.

The challenge—

which one of us could hold our breath the longest
before popping up,
sputtering,
water
escaping our noses,
dribbling
from our barrettes and braids.

We held our heads to the side
and hopped up and down
to let the water seep from our ears.

When the burn in our nostrils faded,
we leaped on top of the water
again and again,
sank,
sprang back up,

took turns holding our hands
underneath each other's backs
teaching each other to
trust the water,
the buoyancy of our bodies.

Eventually we stopped screaming
Don't let me go,

confident enough in ourselves,
the water,
to float.

We doggy-paddled
from the center of the pool to the edge.

Braver, arms outstretched,
eyes closed,
we held our breath
kicked our legs
until we reached the side of the pool.

Eventually I could lie atop
the water's surface on my back,
flutter my arms, until I bumped into someone.

Sorry!

Stand, start again.

Fifth grade.

We have swim class!

I already know how to float. Yes!

Our potbellied teacher stood above us in dry clothing,
demonstrated proper strokes,
stalked the length of the pool with his body hook,
commanded that as we did the breaststroke,
we scooped the water with our hands,
kept a straight line.

As we took turns swimming vertical
or horizontal lengths of the pool,
I was always one of the crooked ones.

You have to open your eyes!

As I floated,
kicked,

stroked,
I could not figure out how to swivel my head,
inhale,
dip head back in the water,
repeat,
stay within the safety dividers.

Open your eyes!

I could not.

Fear of chlorine's sting.

Decades of beauty I could have owned,
gliding above the bottom of pools,
diving under waves,
swimming parallel to shores.

I used to be

angry

my swim teacher
did not request
our parents buy us goggles,
did not set down his pool hook,
get into the pool with us,
and coax me to trust my eyes;

disappointed

in my camp counselors,
sunning their brown bodies to gleaming,

talking to each other
instead of us.

Seasoned now,
I know they were young themselves.

It could have been vanity over hair,
perfumed skin.

Perhaps they were too scared of opening their eyes.

Wise, with means,
I can learn.

Next summer, as classes now are full.

Mami Wata,
please help me find
the flowers, fragrance, jewels,
dances
which please you most.

I implore you,
make me resolute
to open my eyes in the pool.
Learn to breathe through my strokes.

Swim in a straight line.

Threshold

Weeks of planning–
a field trip for my eighth grade social studies class
to visit a replica of the *Amistad*!

During the train ride to South Street Seaport,
my gaze on my chattering progeny of
Puerto Rico,
the Dominican Republic,
Jamaica,
West Africa,
African Americans,
I thought back to my pre-teen self,
Ebony Jr. article about ~~Cinque~~ Sengbe Pieh in my lap.

Every issue I received each month was piled neatly,
unwrinkled, in the stacked crates that were my bookshelves.

Had I had another copy,
I would have cut out the picture of his handsome face,
taped it to my wall,
his brave brown eyes portals to courage.

I had not expected rolling eyes,
sighs,
stiff silence

as the guide walked us around the deck,
pointed to the hold,
relayed the story of the uprising,
the court case.

One girl, who clung to the railing,
then her friend, as we boarded–

Can we go now?

As we walked toward the train station,
I wanted to cry.

In Tribute

Mama Toni Cade Bambara issued the call in 1989–
there is no plaque,
no memorial,
100 million bodies
bellows deep.
We must reclaim those bones.

So every second Saturday of June since then,
some of us descendants of the Maafa
gather along the Coney Island shore.

Face the Atlantic.
Honor the Ancestors.

June 10, 2017, I made the sojourn.

We
everyday women
                and men
                        and children
faith leaders
politicians
                wore or held
        Ileke
        beads
danced   around
        the drummers.

I do not know any West African ceremonial dances.

Stood on the outer ring, feet unmoving at first,
but the djembe commands me.

My
shy
                hips
                        obey

ꙅ
  u
r
  r
e
  n
d
  e
  r

13

And when it was time

to march to the shoreline

I was given a handful
of red and yellow blooms,
blue carnations.

I watched the waves
                    rise
                        peak
                            roll in

Aimed my bouquet as far as I could
towards the horizon.

Whispered words of gratitude
to Brave Ones Whose Names I May Never Know.

A man gently tapped my arm.

Walk away facing the water.
You're not supposed to turn your back on the ancestors.

I took a picture as the sun set.

In the frame,
a woman's afro was a golden halo.

Remnants of blooms washed ashore.

Why Non-Swimmers
Board Boats

To be in motion.

It is why babies love being
swung to sleep.

Some sneer at the subway,
but me?

Hurtling through train tunnels
Bronx to Manhattan,
to Brooklyn or Queens
and back,
pulses me to wary sleep.

Manhattan,
Long walks.
East to west,
north to south.

Circle Line.

Soundtrack as we sail the East River—
lapping water on percussion,
motor's chug on bass,
cars careening the FDR, alto notes.

Skyscrapers shine gold in the sun,
shine silver on cloudy days.

Underbellies of the
Manhattan
Brooklyn
Williamsburg Bridges
menace,
and stand strong.

Off the coast of Massachusetts,
off the coast of Brazil,
I give thanks for
humpback blows,
leaps,
their tails waving farewell.

Oh, to cruise like ducks and swans.

My uneven paddling notwithstanding,
canoeing awakens my fire

trees and mountains

those vivrant things

surrounding me

giving me my breaths

dragonflies whizzing

tickling my ears

tweeting
trilling
as the birds
get where they need to go,
get it on.

Maid of the Mist.
Great cascade of Niagara Falls.

Imagine being that powerful,
that wet
all the time.

Honey,
rock with me.

Dive into my sweet-water cavern,
and dance.

PART II

THE AMBROSE

The Color Red

The Light Ship Ambrose.

Our guide Caleb points to the brick red floor–

They painted the floor red
to remind the sailors of being on land
and keep them from being seasick.
Brick red.
Why not the black-brown or bluish gray
we live on here?
This brick red floor
does not unravel my stomach knot
soften the clump in my throat
as I run my hand
across the felloe and handles of the helm
ease myself through narrow passages
snap photos of the sailors' bunks
as we are lightly rocked
by wind and water.
Red earth,
full of clay minerals,
aluminum and iron oxides,
found in hot climates.
Drains well.
Easy movement of oxygen and carbon dioxide
within the soil.
Where did the boat builders come from?
Did they wipe tears
between red paint brush strokes,
think of palm trees,
fig trees,
azure seas washing ashore,
left-behind family,
long for the days they held
red soil in the palms of their hands?

A Young Sailor Writes Home

My Dearest Love,

I am proud to serve
on the Light Ship Ambrose,
beacon to newcomers
from
Italy
Poland
Russia

but
as I sit here
15 miles from shore
under this lantern's harsh light
sheltering from this wind and beating rain

I confess
everything here is hard

my bunk
clang of the bell
blast of the horn
the crawl of time
the crew swears I will get used to.

They are good men,
serious about our work,
friendly, full of clever stories,
card games,
rough laughter that heats these narrow rooms
but they,
the burn of whiskey,
never clear the thick fog of boredom,
or warm me against this cold night air.

The food–
not wormy hardtack biscuits like the olden days
but not much better-
stirs a sadness in my soul,

a craving for the softness of home,
of you,

your arms around my neck,
the scent of your hair,
the sweet mountains of your bosom,
your tender valleys,

tender meats on my plate,
mashed potatoes with butter,

the tickle in my ears
when you,
when the children, laugh.

Remember you once told me
I don't tell you how much I love you
enough?

When I get home I will.
Every morning when we rise.
Every night before we sleep.

Your Beloved Husband.

A Poet Afloat

I came to the Light Ship Ambrose
to write, certain
clear blue skies,
salt of the sea,
cool breezes,
would move my pen.

After less than an hour,
I am ready to disembark
when again,
my stomach begins to sway.

Shame hovers like a storm cloud.
My ancestors.

Their two to three months
on the Middle Passage.

Makes me wish
for a different kind
of light ship—

a fleet of them,
from the 1500s to the 1800s,

stalking the coastlines,
Senegambia to Angola,

Boston to Charleston
To St. Augustine
To New Orleans

Cuba to Jamaica to Brazil.

Cannons cocked.
Stockpile of rifles,
Machetes.
Ready for war.

Ready to board foul floating tombs.
Unshackle the captured.
Whip, strip the crew naked.

March them down into the hold.

At gunpoint,
force them to lay in and breathe
the piss
the shit

24

the vomit
the blood
the sweat
the tears.

Shackle them.
Ignore their screams,
cries for food or water.

Shove the sick ones,
the rebellious ones into the sea,
the jaws of stealthy sharks.

Dare passing ships
to rescue these wretched thieves.

Though it means
my American foreparents,
and I,
would never
be,

I wish for a fleet of light ships

offering blankets
fresh water
fish
reassurance of safety
impending freedom from captivity.

Sailing under the North Star,

songs of Senegambia to Angola
guiding the way home.

Upon arrival on African shores,
Light Ship crew
would escort
the newly freed
back to their villages.

Oh, to see the joy on the faces of
husbands and wives
sons and daughters
mothers and fathers
sisters and brothers
uncles and aunts
and cousins and
grandparents
that were in mourning.

PART III

THE WAVER TREE

Squall

On one of those tranquil nights

canaries quietly clenching their perches,
dreaming of freely foraging flocks,
Captain Masson nestled in his chair at his table,
smoking his pipe,
staring up at moonglow
through the skylight
at midnight canopy
and its ecstasy of shining jewels across the firmament,

would he have scoffed
if you told him
the Tall Ship Wavertree
would one day be towed into shelter
by a tugboat
named Samson,

that his beloved horn square four-rigger
frequent tramp ship
that carried coal to grain to nitrate to Oregon pine
that circled the great belly of the globe
like a belt three times–
Singapore
Sri Lanka
India
South Africa
Scotland
Canada
New York
Australia
Washington State
Oregon
California
Peru
Uruguay
Brazil
Chile–
would be sold,

be a floating warehouse?

Punta Arenas.

How many sailors
dockworkers
ship captains
tourists
stopped for a moment to be sick to the stomach

as cargo,
then sand,
was loaded and unloaded into and from the hold
of El Gran Valero

and all she could do then was bob by the pier?

How many shed a tear?

I am no great fixer of broken things–

cracked coffee mugs go in the recycle bin,
ripped papers are run through the shredder,
earrings with bent clasps thrown in the trash,
never thread a needle to sew up holes in socks–

but as I sit here on the Wavertree's quarterdeck
warmed by the sun
and chilled by the breeze

it does not matter that
it would not have been cheap
to rebuild in 1910.

They should have re-rigged her mast.
Let the Tall Ship Wavertree sail again.

Honor
        the hands that
        tilled the soil,

that planted the seeds
of cotton
hemp
flax
to weave into canvas,
into sailcloth;

those who stitched
cringles
clews
reefing points,
bolted rope to the sail;

those who sawed and felled great pines
and spruce,
the timber trimmer,
those who shaped and varnished the masts;

the shipbuilders' calloused hands
fingers pierced by splinters
ironworkers operating the furnaces
who smelted iron from its ore,
workers who annealed and quenched and tempered
iron into steel;

the crew who pushed their arms into soreness
walking round the capstan,
those who slipped or fell and
broke their limbs;

the crew who were hit by that hurricane
as the ship headed to Cape Horn,
the three thrown across the deck by sea swells
so hard their legs were broken.

As the Wavertree creaked and limped
towards the Falklands
with storm-battered crew
and shattered mast

did anyone clap,
cheer,

the miracle of her return

climb aboard to greet the crew
cover them with warm blankets?

The Tall Ship Wavertree.
25 years of service.

On one of those tranquil nights
canaries quietly clenching their perches
dreaming freely foraging flocks,
Captain Masson nestled in his chair,
at his table
staring up at moonglow
through the butterfly hatch,
midnight canopy
and its ecstasy of shining jewels across the firmament,

if you told him
The Tall Ship Wavertree,
three-time circumnavigator of the globe,
carrier of 2100 tons,

would be a floating warehouse,
sand barge,
with broken mast,

would he have scoffed,
gone back to smoking his pipe?

PART IV

THE WHITE STAR LINE

The Black Star Line

If I could speak to my great-grandparents,

Papa John
Mama Lula
Papa Milton
Mama Florence,

I would ask if word ever reached them
about *The Negro World*
in rural Kentucky and North Carolina?

Had they heard of The Black Star Line?

Were any of their neighbors
wide-awake men and women
who heard the clock ring,
who sang that the hour had come
to save the race from the burning stake?

Had they, their neighbors, counted their pennies
until they had $5 for a piece of the dream—
to invest in the Black Star Line!

The Black Star Line ships.
For 400,000,000 of us around the world!
To carry people and cargo from
the Americas to a

United States of Africa.

Did
Papa John
Mama Lula
Papa Milton
Mama Florence,

long to go to Harlem
join the crowds standing on piles of logs
on the pier at 135th Street?

Toss their hats and handkerchiefs in the air?

Dance and jump before the Shadyside
set sail up the Hudson?

The New Negro.
The New Soul.
Let us guide our destiny away from the lynch rope and Jim Crow.
Nothing less than liberty!

Did
Papa John
Mama Lula
Papa Milton
Mama Florence
know

the Black Star Line fleet sailed to ports of
Cuba
Costa Rica
Panama
Jamaica

and Black people
rode donkeys and horses
and horse-drawn carts for miles
to witness these ships arrive,

owned and commanded by black men?

Though Marcus Garvey and the UNIA
paid too much for a fleet that was too old,
The Shady Side blew a leak,
The Antonio Maceo blew a boiler that killed a man,

though the Black Star Line fleet never made it to Africa,
and the FBI conspired to get
Marcus Garvey indicted on mail fraud
then deported
with the help of J. Edgar Hoover's black diversity hires—

Herbert Simeon Boulin

Emmett J. Scott
Walter H. Loving
James Wormley Jones

would
Papa John
Mama Lula
Papa Milton
Mama Florence,

have been proud
as I am

that for $5,
so many of us got to own
a piece of a dream.

War

If Captain Smith had to go down with a vessel,
why the Titanic?

Why not the RMS Majestic,
with its
bringing troops
to South Africa during the Boer War?

During this White Man's War,
Boers vs. Brits,

Black South Africans
dug trenches
served as scouts and drivers
delivered messages
raided cattle farms
built forts
guarded ammunition
cared for horses
cooked
gathered firewood
fought in battles.

Scorched earth campaign–

Burned Boer farms.

Black people forced from their lands
to keep them from aiding the Boers.

Internment camps.

Typhoid fever.
Diarrhea.
Dysentery.

Thousands of Black South Africans died.

Black soldiers dumped in unmarked graves.

Then it was
Boers and Brits vs. Africans.

Treaty of Vereeniging.

Black South Africans disenfranchised,
groundwork laid for apartheid.

So
if there were White Star Line ships
that had to sink,

if Captain Smith had to go down with a vessel,
why not the RMS Majestic,

with its bringing troops
to South Africa during the Boer War.

PART V

THE CITY ISLAND SAILBOAT

For the Bronx

Who-ah who-ah
who thinks they're bad!

Who-ah who-ah
who thinks they're bad!

We do!

This poem is for the Bronx.

This poem is for

Donna

Niecy

Tonya

Jimmy

Elsa

Reshemah

Sybil

Dedra

Marla

Jonathan

Wilentz

Mark

Michael

Pam

Lisa

Shareen

Jonathan

Solomon

Jaime

So sad I couldn't sit on the City Island Sailboat,
on the Long Island Sound,

behold

the high rises of my home towering over trees,
tap shoulders of the crew, point,
See? That's where I live!

I'm slim, not short
never smoked Newports!

Snap on me, my home,
if you want to

but my words could cut you
like,
well,
a butterknife.

I just couldn't be *that* mean.
Too busy having fun.

Slam of our screen doors
as we ran in and out of the house
for sips of soda and water,
bathroom breaks,

to switch out our bikes
for roller skates
or a deck of cards
for Spit or Spades.

Kickball—
tree, first base, lamppost, second base, tree, third base.

Niecy and Tonya's stoop was home!

Rode my skateboard
until a pebble stopped my wheels,
sent me tumbling

peroxide/iodine/band aid—
I'm fine!

Fine enough to blow your mind!
Tag!
Red light-green light-1-2-3!
You think you're fast,
but you won't catch me!

Echo of clackers across the courtyard
but by God, don't let them hit your hands!

We threw bang snaps on the ground
around the 4th of July

double Dutch ropes
and flying feet whipping concrete
1up 23456789
2up 2346789

Double orange.
Double apple.

Hopscotch.
Keys and pebbles as markers.
Keep off that sidewalk crack!
Don't break your mama's back!

Teen girls
swinging keys
as we hip-twitched
to the candy store,
the supermarket,
when Mommy or Daddy told us to
pick up the rice or chicken for dinner.

For the fellas hanging out
around the shopping center–

My name?
Mind your B.I. business!

The smell of fresh cut grass.

Songs
   of sparrows
   robins
   mourning doves nestled high in the trees
   bouncing across the ground
   flying back and forth across our window sills.

Music everywhere–

      Michael Jackson
      Chaka Khan
      Marvin Gaye
      George Clinton
      Sade

      low blast of the horns of the Amtrak trains

      blunka-blunk-blunka-blunk-blunka-blunk
      of the wheels on the tracks

      the pitter patter of rain

      Us, sitting at our windows,
      drumming our fingers
      wondering when it was going to stop
      and when it did, like the
      earthworms, we came out for air,
      our noses and lungs full of petrichor

We stood on our shoreline,
our gaze on Goose Island,
how the bay flowed into City Island Sound.

Who could throw rocks the farthest?
Hit the water the hardest?
Never me, but gave it my BX best.

Yeah, this poem is for the borough
that made me,

      that Robert Moses,

      the Cross Bronx Expressway,

      and arson fires

      could not kill,

for the people who think the borough

with the most parkland in New York City,

that birthed

library lions Patience and Fortitude on 42nd and Fifth,

Haagen Dazs ice cream,

salsa,

hip hop,

is a wasteland of flying bullets.

Who-ah who-ah
who thinks they bad?

Who-ah who-ah
who thinks they bad?

I do!

Free Spirit

Girlhood to womanhood,
that motor hum of speed boats racing
under Pelham Bay Bridge
to Goose Bay,
back to City Island,
had me dreaming about sitting
beneath a sail.

And I here I am on City Island Harbor,
pink pen in hand,
writing in my notebook,
buildings in my neighborhood
like arms stretched up to the skyline,

$75 in my wallet,
$3 in my checking account,
after the rent is paid.

A friend of Brad,
a lovely woman named Neela,
has allowed me to sit on her sailboat.

Fred, a really nice guy,
brought me out on his launch boat.

On The Free Spirit,
being a free spirit,
this steely blue cloudy day.

Local meteorologists promise
it is not going to rain.

Another sailboat passes by, driven by a woman.
I wonder what she does for a living,

what any of these boat owners
do for a living,
to afford a sailboat,
its upkeep.

But I have done this much of my life,
seeking spaces and experiences
my socioeconomic status might prohibit.

When Freddy first dropped me off,
I almost begged him not to leave me,
but now
as I sit here doing something just for me

crepuscular rays
spreading sun glitter across the water,
aromatic, soft breeze
on my head and arms,
soul-soothing, light rocking of the boat,
I am not seasick.

I am safe in this aloneness,
this quiet
punctuated by

Freddy's motor as he makes his rounds.

Machines in the boatyard.

A bell on a buoy.

An airplane overhead.

I take pictures of the City Island shoreline.
Piers.
Sailboats.
Rocks.
Bay Terrace houses lining the shoreline.
The arch of the Whitestone Bridge.
High rises in Queens and Westchester
standing tall in the distance.

How I love the water
especially beaches

southern Atlantic coast,
Caribbean.
That greenish, turquoise water.

This water in this harbor,
the bay,
Long Island Sound,
a murky jade.

There is beauty anyway.

Here in the Bronx.

Chirping birds.
No honking horns,
revving car engines.

A gull has just skimmed the water.
Flown off.

What is was like before
the Dutch West India Company,
before massacres like Pound Ridge,
before Thomas Pell bought his 50,000 acres,

when
the Lenape lived here,
growing maize,
fishing,
gathering oysters and clams,
collecting shells
for wampum?

What did their houses look like?

What kinds of boats
did they build and sail,
which shade of blue
were these waters,

before they were colonized,
industrialized,
polluted?

To think developers
wanted a commercial center
to rival Manhattan around here.
Ha.

Hart Island, to my left.
I google it.
A million bodies rest there.

Inmates from Rikers
used to make 37 cents an hour
as pall bearers and grave diggers.

Besides
a tuberculosis sanitorium,
a prison,
psychiatric hospital,
other dumping grounds
for the marginalized,

it housed a training ground and barracks
for black soldiers during the Civil War–
31st Infantry Unit of U.S. Colored Troops.

On the southern tip of Hart Island,
Solomon Riley
wanted to build a summer resort on Hart Island–
a Negro Coney Island–
a triumph over whites-only amusement parks
in Rye and Dobbs Ferry.

After a boardwalk,
bathing pavilion,
eight boarding houses,
a dance hall
were built on his four acres,
before the grand opening on July 4, 1925,

white supremacy spit on Black independence,
Black dreams.

Claiming fears of escape attempts from prisoners,
the city had the land condemned,
bought the land back from Riley.

And in that part of Hart Island,
they buried victims of AIDS.

Julia de Burgos.
A pauper's death.

This world, and what it does with poets.
Women of stature.

They had to cut off her legs
to fit her in the coffin,
people whispered.

She must have visited her family and friends
in their dreams.

Come get my body.
Send me home to Puerto Rico.

Every beautiful place harbors
sad songs.

A cold breeze
makes me shudder,
put on my jacket.

I have been out here almost two hours,
and nature calls.

I call Fred for my pick up,
though I hate to leave my seat
on the water

under steely-blue, cloudy sky
competing with the sun,

the red-orange rustic majesty
of changing leaves
along the shore.

MORE FROM THIS AUTHOR

If you enjoyed this book, please check out these other titles from

Carla M. Cherry:

iiPublishing

Gnat Feathers and Butterfly Wings
Thirty Dollars and a Bowl of Soup
Honeysuckle Me
These Pearls Are Real
Stardust and Skin
May He Bless My Name

Grandma Moses Press

Clap Your Hands, Stomp Your Feet

Finishing Line Press

Sundays and Hot Buttered Rolls: A Granddaughter of Harlem Speaks

Please visit Ms. Cherry's website:
https://www.carlacherrybxpoet1.com/

If you would like to reach Ms. Cherry,
you are welcome to email her at:

carlacherrybxpoet@gmail.com

BIOGRAPHY

Carla M. Cherry is a veteran high school English teacher. Her work has appeared in *Random Sample Review, Anti-Heroin Chic, La Libreta, ISLE,* and *Raising Mothers*. A Best of the Net and Pushcart Prize nominee, she has authored six books of poetry, *Gnat Feathers* and *Butterfly Wings, Thirty Dollars and a Bowl of Soup, Honeysuckle Me, These Pearls Are Real, Stardust and Skin,* and *May He Bless My Name* (iiPublishing), and two other chapbooks: *Clap Your Hands, Stomp Your Feet* (Grandma Moses Press) and *Sundays and Hot Buttered Rolls: A Granddaughter of Harlem Speaks* (Finishing Line Press). She holds an M.F.A. in Creative Writing from the City College of New York.

www.ingramcontent.com/pod-product-compliance
Lightning Source LLC
Chambersburg PA
CBHW061716120626

46550CB00003B/1244

9798985020489